73

MultiVerse

ༀ

Edited by Rob Sturma and Ryk McIntyre

Write Bloody Publishing
America's Independent Press

Austin, TX

WRITEBLOODY.COM

MultiVerse

© 2014 Write Bloody Publishing

Write Bloody
First Edition
ISBN: 9781938912542

Cover art by Ashley Siebels
Proofread by Helen Novielli
Edited by Rob Sturma and Ryk McIntyre
Interior layout by Ashley Siebels

Type set in Bergamo from www.theleagueofmoveabletype.com

Printed in Tennessee, USA

Write Bloody Publishing
Austin, TX
Support Independent Presses
writebloody.com

To contact the author, send an email to writebloody@gmail.com

MADE IN THE USA

MultiVerse

An Anthology of Superhuman Proportions

MULTIVERSE

An Anthology of Superhuman Proportions

FOREWORD (EARTH-ONE)

In the 1990s I ran a small comic book store. This is not a dream, or a hoax, or an imaginary story. But that isn't where this starts. When I was a kid, every summer spent in Maine with my cousins involved a fair amount of pretending to be superheroes. I think I usually pretended to Batman, unless we were swimming, and then I was Aquaman. Duh.

Another thing that meant summer for me was the annual Justice League/Justice Society crossover. My eyes could hardly contain it... we're talking two Batmans (Earth 1 and Earth 2), two of Superman, The Flash, Green Lantern, Wonder Woman, plus several more that did not have direct counterparts, like Wildcat or J'onn J'onnz, the Martian Manhunter...THE POINT IS, you had literally a few dozen heroes in one book. I never have forgotten that pure sense of kid-wonder, a thing I can still feel to this day.

Flash-forward to that comic book store I used to run. There I learned to hate comics, mostly due to the "collector craze" of the mid-1990s where comics were viewed as short-term get-rich-quick investments, and the ill-informed were duped into buying glittery crap by greedy publishers. People were spending stupid money based on the covers of comic books. They weren't even READING them. And pretty much every cliché of comic nerd-dom being populated chiefly by sexist, racist, homophobic, pale, pale boys was accurate, so far as my customer base went. I loved when the few dedicated female customers came in to shop and talk, but felt bad for the way they were leered at or mocked by the boys club. I said "Balls to that!" and my store yearned to become a place where people who loved stories and characters could meet. We even tried to sell books without pictures.

The store closed not long after that.

But recently I have witnessed the emergence of other voices and talents in the industry that are shattering the hegemony of the White Male. Creators and characters of diverse genders, sexual identity, race and nationalities, et cetera. Makes me want to open that store back up again... almost.

It is those two spirits, the childlike awe of the superhero and a desire for a collection of voices that mirror every anybody that reads comics, which drove this anthology. Years ago, I was involved in a well-received but commercially failed anthology called Look! Up in the Sky! that tried to do the same thing in its clumsy, poorly laid-out way. But it is enough to me that it informed, to some tiny extent (maybe only a Ray Palmer's worth, but still), this collection of poems.

Come on in. The stories are fine and there is room for everyone, especially you.

--Ryk McIntyre

FOREWORD (EARTH-616)

Seems you can't throw an irradiated playing card these days without hitting a superhero. The nerds of yesterday have become the tastemakers of today, and our media is flush with extraordinary beings on our TV screens, movie theaters, and all over the internet. Stan Lee is the Godfather of cameos and cool, and his True Believers are legion. Superheroes have been dissected and deconstructed, and the rest of the world is learning what some of us have known for years: There's a heaping helping of humanity underneath the masks, capes, and gadgetry. Of course the best stories always start with the roots of Joseph Campbell and the hero's journey, but the generations that grew up on Jack Kirby's bold brushstrokes have seen, or proactively added, a lot of nuance to their favorite meta-human champions.

All of this is just to say that superheroes are rad, everyone has a favorite, and I think the heroes we gravitate toward speak to how we perceive ourselves, or perhaps who we wish we could be. As soon as I knew what angst was, boy did Spider-Man become a shining beacon of hope for me. On days when I felt ugly and unlovable, I totally got where The Thing was coming from. I was a voracious reader from an early age, but comic books helped me learn faster and more completely. I remember reading issues of Green Lantern/Green Arrow and feeling the weight of racism as Hal Jordan was called out on helping every color of skin except the brown skins. I watched Gwen Stacy (and over the years, so many other characters) meet her fate and felt the frustration and loss when her knight in shining webbing couldn't save her. I didn't just grow up with comic books and superheroes; they grew up with me.

So here we are, living in a world where you can be Batman on the Xbox and where comic creators are working hard to keep representation alive in the four-color but often white-washed world. Muslim-American Ms. Marvel from Jersey City? Yes please. Batwoman is queer and Jewish? Outstanding. It's a good time to be a nerd, and we're here to celebrate this one amazing aspect of what we love. Here's to the heroes, some more obvious than others. Here's to their arch-nemeses. Here's to the people caught in between, and here's to the poetry in all of it. For every time you wished you could fire a signal into the night to see if someone would save you, Ryk and I hope these poems will make things right again.

Onward, dear Readers. Onward.

—Rob Sturma

AFTER THE END OF THE WORLD

by *Victor Infante*

Image from childhood sketchpad:
    superhero, cape flowing in the stellar breeze,
        fingers that twist girders
            dug into meteor,
                floating in space.

Second frame, expanded view:
    he's on his knees, amid the rubble
        of a shattered planet, tears
            that should stream down his face
                frozen to icicles.

In the background, the Statue of Liberty –
    recognizable landmark, adrift in the vacuum,
while the superhero surveys with eyes that
    see the nuclei of atoms, that watch electrons
        buzz in endless orbits. No dialogue –
            in space, no one can hear
                your exposition.

And I'd wonder if Lady Liberty
    would float like Voyager through endless night,
        or if the lack of gravity would rip rivet from rivet –
            and I'd wonder what kept invulnerable skin
                wrapped tight around invulnerable bone;
                    what it means for breathing
                        to be a habit; if in that moment
                            he'd simply stop.

And I'd wonder how the superhero
    arrived at this moment, did he flash
        like lightning across the sky, racing
            proton torpedoes mere inches
                from his outstretched hand?

Or perhaps it was heartbreak; letter left on the nightstand
    from Girl Friday gone for quieter weekends,
        and in his rage he pounded the ground so hard
            as to split the Earth's mantle, until his shattering
            and the planet's
                were indistinguishable.

And perhaps humanity was out there, somewhere –
        enslaved to alien tyrants who banished them to endless mine shafts,
            or adrift across dimensions, stuttering lost and mad
                    in the alleys of worlds that resemble their own, except
                        small details – they cannot name the president,
                            the capitol of Pennsylvania.

And perhaps the superhero eventually finds them,
        plucks them from banishment, leads them across
the deserts of space, where they wander
        for 40 days and 40 nights, until they arrive
            at some ripe planet
                    the hero cannot enter.

Or perhaps they're simply vanished, extinction
        recorded on quivering lips, and the superhero
            disappears into the Heavens, gone, until
                    he and they are merely constellations, faint outlines
                        in the sky, some remembrance of lines
                            drawn between stars.
                                I only know that this
                                    is where the story always starts.

JOKER: YEAR ONE

by Geoff Kagan Trenchard

-October 30th-

It's been months of days at the library.
Learning all there is to know about
how to make napalm from Nerf foam
mixed with lighter fluid,
the Zimbardo Prison Experiment,
and the Gotham City PD's standard procedures
in case of natural disaster or terrorist attack.
Soaks it up like fresh gauze.

Years of weeks in the city dump.
Shooting strays with assault rifles
so his arms grow accustomed to recoil.
Sparring with winos until he can drive
a hood ornament through an eye socket
in one smooth action.

In his room, explosions in bloom
are tacked on all the walls. In the center
he sits cross legged. Holds his hand
a few inches above a portable blowtorch.
Learns to keep it there
just a little longer each time.

-January 13th-

After the third liquor store, realizes he might as well
just walk in with the gun out. It's the way he moves
through the room. Dogs shudder, children cry, plants wince.
Even without the make-up, even before they see the scars,
the victim knows something sharp and wet is about to happen.

After the fourth stash house, decides regular crews
are for regular crooks. When they leave him in the Narrows,
icy boots ringing his ears, snow sticking to his bloody lips,
he vows to not work with anyone
he doesn't plan on shooting.
Smirks at how quick
a broken face teaches a lesson.

-April 1st-

He's been up for days. Eyes sunk
back like eight balls, teeth rotting yellow
with plaque, hands rattling in happy jitters.

It was supposed to be a quick penthouse invasion
over Easter weekend but things got complicated.

You would be surprised how many
so-called "bad men" get skittish
when Grandma starts to gargle
from a box cutter slice cross the wind pipe.
How a hardened criminal just melts
at the first application of a hot stovetop.

Guys like that never understand.
It's not about the money,
it's about the half-second

when the prey's eyes
turn from terror wide
to numb thin.

It will be Tuesday morning soon.
There is a hundred dollar
meat cleaver in the kitchen
that has yet to be used to split a bone.

He knows he's on to something,
but hasn't found a face
for it yet. Can't decide
on what shape the ghost
of this story should take.

A little girl's muffled scream
shakes through duct tape. Blood
back splatters an arching smile
on her cheek. He thinks yes, yes,
this is the look we are going for.

-July 3rd-

Birth certificate, social security card and every picture
ever taken of him are ash in the bottom of a bath tub.
Remembers last summer, before all this all started
when he first heard the rumor about the demon
that haunts the wicked. Still has the newspaper
clipping. Mob boss splayed on a searchlight
like a split chicken. Keeps it folded in
his breast pocket. A love letter.
Wanted poster. Report card
to aspire to.

Hones the edge of his knives and bullets
for tonight's double homicide robbery.

Plays solitaire with his calling cards.
The ones people weed out of the deck
when they want to keep the game predictable.

-September 27th-

Standing on the corner of Fifth and Main waiting
for disposable accomplices the mask dangles
from his fingers like a severed head.

Truck screeches to a halt, he gets in,
barely able to contain the laughter.

This is the end of the beginning.

STEPPING INTO ROGUE

by Stevie Edwards

Let's try this:
I don't think you should touch me.

The first boy I kissed wound up in a coma.
My hands are bad tools, weapons—they take more
than I can control. They control without asking.
I can't promise it won't happen again. I took his
childhood, his mind's eye, his life force inside me
for a while. Couldn't stop it.

    (That is a story. This is the truth: I first kissed a boy in a photo booth at a roller-skating
    rink. I lied and told him he wasn't my first. His mother found him dead at home, his
    air all choked out, an asthma inhaler flopped on the floor. The second boy I kissed
    tried to kill himself on Christmas Eve after I came to his home with a tray of holiday
    cookies and kissed him goodbye in the doorframe while my mom waited in the
    minivan. Last I heard, he manages a Walgreens in a Detroit suburb. I try to imagine
    him liking it.)

I don't think you should touch me.
I have a gift. It means
alienation. I have a curse. It means duty, heavy
luggage that is always mine to carry.

Is it working? How about this:
I'll dye my hair with the gray streak
I've surely earned.
Would it be better
if I wore a yellow cat-suit with green accents
so you can see who I really am
from far away? Would it be
better if I made up a new name? Call me *Rogue,*
Call me *Babe,* Call me *Bitch*—it might feel good.
Does it? When I move out
and take your favorite blue-rimmed plates,
when I give our bed to the sub-letters to seal the deal.

I don't think you should touch me. I break.
I ruin. I am not a villain. I am nobody's heroine.

MILE-A-MINUTE

by Curtis X Meyer

They they always wanna know if I'm fa-faster than Superman. You you can't clock me. Know how much I eat in a single setting? 10 large pizzas. 12 hot dogs. 36-and-a-half cheeseburgers. Box of donuts. 7-layer cake. Enough to kill you. I just burn it off. Leave buffets looking like graveyards. My mind's on constant marathon. My blood cells are hot rods on the Autobahn. My life is perpetual bullet time. I watch snowflakes suspended in midair. My pulse is permanent heart attack. My pulse is the wing of a hummingbird on crack. Speed. 5 shots of espresso. They they always wanna know if I'm fa-faster than Superman. Superman is a bug on my windshield. Gravity is no excuse. Can't fly. Run up walls. Can't talk to fish. Run on water. Shoot up tornadoes like staircases. Bricks. Birdhouses. Mailboxes become stepping stones. I'm so fast I can circle the globe. Come back. Kick myself in the back of the head. (Totally happened. Simple physics. Don't ask how.) I tend to speed-read. They called Navajos Wind-talkers in World War II. Know where the term whipper-snapper comes from? That's what they called cowboys too young to hold guns. Cowboys and Indians. The crack of a whip is its tip breaking the sound barrier. Tha-tha-that's the sound I make when I get up in the morning. Brush my teeth. Shower. Wait for water. Raindrops aren't drop-shaped. They're circles. Read that once. Now I see see them. Dodge dodge them. Zig-zig-zigzagging. Buzzing is the sound of a bee's wings. Bees can't fly. They're unsound aerodynamically. That's untrue. Bees' wings move in circles. Like propellers. So do birds'. I see see them now. You think I'm re-re-repeat-peating myself. This is my voi-voi-voice catching up to the s-s-sound sound barrier. Jiffies are real things. Units of time. Back in a jiffy. Simple physics. A train leaves Metropolis going 50 miles per hour. Not strong as than Superman. I hit once, say Hi to a freight train. I poke a thousand times a second, you're being pecked to death by hummingbirds. Faster than fast. Faster than faster. Faster than a speeding bullet. Why bulletproof when you can dodge missiles? They all know me in the city. Breezes at the back of their necks. They say the suit's ostentatious. Bright red. Gold lightning bolt. Say no camouflage did in the redcoats. I say the redcoats weren't fast enough. This suit ain't a STOP sign. It's a challenge: I dare you to stop me. Not super-strong. Simple physics. Love to tell you more. It'd be too fast. You don't have the time. I mean, it'd take too long. I've got all the time in the world. I mean, here:

I can slow it down for you. But it hurts reducing myself to your level. I can feel my teeth vibrating in my jaw. My molars are jackhammers drilling into my gums so I

hafta keep talking like this. Know how lonely it is waiting for everyone else to catch up? I can serve myself in tennis. All your small-talk looks like glaciers playing golf. I'm not talking too fast. Your A.D.D. is my snooze button. You're think think thinking too slow. Know know know how boring it is saving the world? I fight giant robots with lasers. Save kids from burning buildings. Kittens from trees. Load old ladies' groceries. Eat. Drink. Take a bathroom break. All before the first robot fires a shot. The rest of the League tell me, relax. I need a vacation. Where would I go I haven't already been? Had tacos in Baja. Dim sum in Hong Kong. Love to go clubbing. Your music puts me to sleep. Drum n' Bass is my lullaby. Can't stand museums. Never got statues or still life. I find the voice of auctioneers oddly soothing. My family. I hafta. Have   to. My family. They help slow things   down. My wife   kisses me   like time

stopping. Next thing,

I'm gone. Hafta keep running. Can't outrun Fear. So I run towards it. The definition of Courage. I'm not fast. I'm brave. I'm not fast. I'm beyond. I'm beyond beyond. I'm beyond your beyondest idea of beyond. Faster than fast. Can't let Life catch me. Can't let Death catch catch up to me. This is this is

how fa-fa-fa-fast I am.

EVERYBODY IS SPIDERMAN

by Robbie Q. Telfer

Painting yourself into a corner
isn't an issue if you're
Spiderman except Spiderman
has spent his whole existence
becoming more and more like
Spiderman so that at this point
even if he wanted to stop being
Spiderman, he couldn't –
this is the problem with being
fictional and written by
everybody. Everybody is
Spiderman. Like one day
he's going to be like *Hey guys,*
I decided to become a bus driver.
Everybody – who is also Spiderman
mind you – would be like *No way,*
man, you gotta be Spiderman forever.
> *Yeah but the process for becoming a*
> *bus driver is actually pretty elaborate –*
> *they get like 1000 applications a month.*
So like, you expect people to give their
fare to a guy in a skin-tight…
> *No, I'm… well… I'm ACTUALLY*
> *Peter Parker.*
Fool, we know you're Peter Parker,
we can read that part of the comic
too. Everybody knows you're
Peter Parker. Everybody is
Peter Parker.
> *But don't you also see then*
> *that I'm splitting my identity*
> *all the time? I feel like I'm*
> *the mask more than the man.*
Hey, you can make a mask out of anything
if you poke out eye holes. A comic book
can be a mask.
> *The bus?*
Just poke out eye holes. That's it.
We're gonna pick you up, poke out
eye holes in your torso and we're
all going to wear a Peter Parker
mask and we will be known as
PeterParkerman and our superpower
is that we replaced being Spiderman

with ennui and a bus driver's
uniform, and we will sit in the
living rooms of evil doers shaking
our heads from side to side and
asking a lot of questions we don't
listen to the answers of and we
will overstay our welcome and
eat all of their honey-roasted
peanuts and we will defeat evil
by complicating their understanding
of evil. PeterParkerman will
wonder how he got to this point
100% of the time and he'll
stop shaving because what's
the point. Everybody is PeterParkerman.
We all wear masks on top of our masks…
Shut up, Spiderman, we're over it.

DITKO'S DAY

by Chad Parentau

Wake up, walk kitchen
measure cereal box,
empty next shopping day,
last month's pages
as table mat.

Kitchen, bedroom, bathroom
no more than once, planning
eye's path to drawing table,
composed as splash page.

Visit Kirby cove,
whisper it's too late,
take business card.
use marker, blot half-black.
Hold white side to hand back.

Go home, stare out
window till night
fall. Spider-Man musical
next door.

Put on white suit,
find backstage, sneak
up scaffolding, each step
no trick. Peer over,

watch unearned star's
inevitable misstep. Witness
his fall from grace.

DIANA PRINCE WHERE ARE YOU...

by Leigh White

The glitter
is stuck to her tongue
making kissing more of an exfoliation
The gold is in her veins stays mostly in her upper torso
Because it's more like a cabin, a place to get away, a place to build fires
The invisible is deep inside her heart
Because she doesn't want anyone to see her stutter with emotion,
or fall into the gravity of want
The lasso stays on her left hip, coiled neatly
It knows its place
Her shiny bracelets are mirrors of the wrong,
masters of the ricochet,
and forged to keep her blood inside her wrists
Her eyeglasses are missing,
again

SECRET IDENTITY

by Gus Wood

Clark,
when you run to those phone booths,
shirt-buttons skittering to the pavement
as they burst from your chest,
do you make a point of changing fast enough
for no one to see you?
Dressed in your red and blue regalia,
"S" on your chest like a badge of honor,
everyone clapping and cheering the man
you were born to be,
I just have to know what that's like.

There is a super hero,
bubbling underneath my shirt,
hiding shy in the seams of my jeans,
I call him "perfect."
But the monsters of my metropolis
will headline him "crossdresser," "freak."
Do you know what they did
to the last boy in tights?

So I really need to know,
was it the sun, the fall from Krypton,
what made you leap tall buildings,
stop speeding trains, and outrace bullets?
Was it just the fact that you could do it all
unencumbered by the lead weight
of trying to be human,
in the clothes you were born to wear?

Silk blouse, sheer stockings,
stuffed under graphic tee and hiking boots,
hoping no one can spot my secrets,
the bulging different under my normal life.
Shame is feeling a lot like Kryptonite these days.
It's killing me, Clark.

I do not have your luxury
of having my clothes wrapped around me
like swaddling clothes on the day
you were found in Kansas.
Instead I pick them like forbidden fruit
from department store trees
when no one is looking long enough
for me to sneak away with something
in a color I actually like.

Clark Kent, Superman, Kal-El, Last Son of Krypton
you have so many names,
but only one uniform.
Tell me, is there agony
on your side of the spectrum as well,
You and I, Clark, we both need costumes
to be ourselves.
Did it take you long to grow into yours?
Until you could move mountains,
save lives, stay as strong as you are,
how long before you could change
in a phone booth and leave your shame ringing
like the unending dial-tone of the phone
you left hanging off the hook?

Tell me, Superman,
how do I wear what I want
and still be invincible?
How do I stop bullets
when they are fired from whispers and sideways glances?
Tell me, Clark, please,
how long before Lois
let you wear the cape
to bed?

WHEN PETER PARKER CRASHES AT YOUR PLACE

by Dalton Day

Don't mention your arachnophobia.
Don't refer to the internet
as "the web," and then look at him expecting a laugh.

Leave the jokes to him.

Close all the windows.
Draw all the blinds. Offer him a drink,
and ask him about Mary Jane.

He won't answer.

When he starts to cry, don't ask him if he's okay.
Don't try and change the subject by
talking about all your responsibilities at work.

Don't talk about responsibility.

Let him hold his head in his hands.
When he excuses himself to the bathroom, you will hear
him break your bathroom mirror. Let him.

He'll ask you if he can just go to bed,
and he'll apologize for not talking as much as usual.

Give him blankets.

Pretend you don't see the blood coming
through his shirt, or the bruises on his face.

Tell him goodnight.
Tell him you'll see him in the morning.

And no matter what, don't ask him to stick around.

LOVE LETTER AFTER
THE END OF THE WORLD

by Heather Knox

for Zak

Guess we saved it. Earth.
Call me pretty bird,
your Black Canary.
It's you that I heart, and more,
my zerospace, my afterdark.

They said it wouldn't last,
the end or us or the time
ante-hero. Unmasked we're too fragile
and small for their world.
Ask anyone in a hospital gown.

Look out the window.
See how the other windows glow?
Look up. Love, all those stars are dead light.
Trace their patterns on the pane
with your fingertip. I'll do the same
with your scars, constellate with mine:
someone a long time from now
will point and tell our story,

how the end came and went.
How it was dark for 11 AM,
and ice, everything.
How for an apocalypse
it came on very natural:
dark and ice and doomsayers
and the Justice League bickering.
The perk of being unmasked
is not needing a phone booth,
not needing to change to stay the same.

Post-apocalyptically speaking,
I'm still, always, yours. So suit up.
Quiver-and-arrow up,
my knight unarmored.
By your side I'll Canary Cry
and *I love you*
until my voice breaks.

SIDEKICKS

by Scott Woods

The old professor who crooks the wisdom knot at the back of his
        head on the cool metal of a coffee shop windowsill
        and remembers an old Tuscany in May

the two kids skipping school
        to play the last Pac-Man console in the
        last greasy pizzeria in town
with lunch money and high score dreams

the sister-girl prayer group and Thursday night closet book club
the Livingston Avenue jump-rope championship squad
the boys playing pirates in treasure-less dust
the three-legged dog that hates water
the prostitute's last leg-up
the lippy boy in the mall
the old
the park bench warmers
the pigeon feeders
that one girl.

When the guy in the red cape
smashes the ten-foot alien through an office building
with a nearby Cadillac
it is almost never like you see in comic books –

broken glass
flying bricks
four-colored astonishment and awe.

Nothing vaporizes.
Everything finds a place to land, to be.

When you live in a world where people in their
pajamas break things daily to forestall tragedy,
the irony is never lost on those of us left behind
who don't wear masks to work.

You either walk around loving everyone or no one.
Glass must rest its wings.
Bricks must pocket themselves somewhere warm.

The school teacher who happens to die in battle,
screaming from behind the wheel of a used Nissan Fox
as all her car payments end in the
name of truth and justice,
the papers will call her a victim.

We stopped trying to convince them otherwise years ago.
Those of us who walk in the shadow of human landmines
and blonde bombshells that actually explode
and capes that drape thick necks like holy flags,
those of us who make our way in
slow, people time,
we do not call them victims.
We call them sidekicks.

Aileen Wuornos is known as America's first female serial killer. She murdered eight men, all of whom she met while working as a prostitute. She claimed that each murder was in self-defense against men who had raped or attempted to rape her. She later reversed her claim, and was executed by the State of Florida in 2002.

William Marston, the creator of Wonder Woman, was also the inventor of the modern lie detector test.

EXECUTED SERIAL KILLER AILEEN WUORNOS PREPS WONDER WOMAN FOR THE POLYGRAPH

by Joanna Hoffman

Whatever you do, don't get nervous. If you're shaking, it's all a lie, even if it's true. First they're gonna ask your name. I was Aileen, and Sandra, and Susan, and Cammie, and Lori. Some of these were a lie, but I can't tell you which ones. Some days I caught my reflection in the mirror and stopped cold, reaching for the gun; woke up in my lover's arms furious that she was holding someone else while I slept.
Next, they'll ask you if you remember the night it happened. What they mean is, do you remember the version of a story that they believe to be true? When they talk, you have to listen to the syllables under the floorboards. Honesty is just another mask. I told them yeah, I remember that night. They asked me if I thought I was in danger. I said yes. This was not a lie but it wasn't the truth either. Yes, there is a carousel of snakebite and hate spinning in my chest, a roulette of every man's face who held me down and slapped me when I cried. That night, the needle landed on him. That night, he smelled like my grandfather's basement, like my brother's casket, like the sweaty rag he stuffed into my mouth to keep me from screaming. Two of those things are a lie, wanna guess?

When they ask if you knew what was going on, tell them you had a lasso of truth but it got you nothing in the end, that you knew by then you were never writing the story anyway, that this was just happening and you were drawn into it. You seemed so sweet, how you followed your man to the ends of the earth. No one thought you'd end up here. I know what love is, too, you know. Everything I ever did I did for her. When she called me crying from that hotel room, of course I knew the wires were tapped. Why else would I have confessed like that, unless I knew they had my girl? I would do it again and again. You're no different.

When they ask you if you feel sorry, try not to laugh. Say you're sorry for all of it, that you were crushed into a skeleton you could never fit into. That you were given the power of speech but someone else's language, that your whole life had to fit into neatly drawn squares. If you laugh, it's all over. If you cry, good, but don't overdo it. Honest people sniffle, but don't sob. Honest people wipe their eyes and look embarrassed when they cry. Trust me, I know these things.

When they ask you if you'd do it again, swallow hard. Think about what will come of this. Who cares what the truth is, if all that matters is what you want? They want the monster slain, and you just want to rest. Tell them sure, whatever it takes. But you won't even get that far. It'll all be over after they ask you your name.

SUPERMAN USES HIS FINGERS TO COUNT OFF THE THINGS HE'S NOT AFRAID OF

by Rich Boucher

Let's see, here:

I'm not afraid of bullets, so that's one thing;
I guess I'll use my left thumb to remember bullets.
Bulletproof equals not afraid of bullets.

Fire doesn't seem to do anything to me,
so let's say fire is my left index finger, then.

I got hit by a train once, and if I recall correctly,
it smarted a little bit, but that's about it.
My left middle finger for the locomotive.

Lex Luthor is a pain, but I think honestly
that he's really just crazy jealous and can't let shit go.
He knows a lot about me, but I'm a pretty easy-to-read guy.
He should go on my left ring finger.

Left pinky. Super-strong Russian gorillas.
A lot of people would be afraid of super-strong Russian gorillas.
Not me, though, I'm Superman, for Christ's sake.
Come at me, super-strong Russian gorilla-bros.

When this Earth's Sun eventually dies out
I'll probably have some big problems to deal with
but I doubt I'll live into my millions of years.
Yeah, the Sun dying would be bad for me,
but I'm not afraid of it, so that goes on my right thumb.

I'm totally not afraid of werewolves and vampires.
I mean, maybe I *should* be, but I'm just not.
I kind of don't even care about them that much.
Right index finger.

So glad my natural invulnerability affords me
protection against the whole host of human diseases:
middle finger to cancer, just like the humans do.

That time I got stuck at the bottom of the ocean
for a week straight underneath that luxury liner?
A hassle for sure, but it's not like I could ever *drown* or anything.
Right ring finger for drowning.

Right pinky finger. What's the last thing I would be afraid of?
Oh, yes, *heights.* I don't have any reason to be afraid of heights.
I can fly, so even if I fell off the Empire State Building,
I could probably just start to fly about halfway down…

…wait a minute.

What if I fell off the Empire State Building
but I was asleep at the time?

I wonder if it's true what they say about dying in your dreams.

NO MATTER THE ENDING,
THE BEGINNING IS LIGHT

by Patricia Smith

Alison "Ali" Blaire, AKA "The Disco Dazzler," was a sometimes member of the X-Men in the early 1980s. Her "power" was turning noise into a light show. In other words, she was a human disco.

Every woman knows that the only way to make a man see truth--
to bear witness to its insistent bleed and dangling edges-- is to blind
him. Make him know the hollow triumph of crawling toward sound
and teaching his thick fingertips to grasp light. If you wrong me, boy,
I'll be the phosphorescent thump at the back of your head, the drum
confounding your pulse, I will *own* your eyes. I'll be your absolute
dance floor, oil shine and shard, and the rest of your days will be spent
praying for the return of your spine, all of you will be whirl and hip.
You will exist only on and within me, as you are slowly ripped wide
by balls of splintered mirror and the maddening looped bridge of lyric,
the cadence will reverse you until you are meat and heartbeat beneath
my wheels. And when you are one breath away from emptied, I will
open my purpled maw and warble a song that is just for you, a loving
and patient screech layered over patented sixteenths on the high hats,
until you and your crime drizzle like sweat through the floorboards.
As your blood brothers scan the wreckage, bellowing your name,
I plan to demurely sparkle. All I did was dazzle you toward shadow.
I pumped the volume, led you onto a smooth surface. All anyone will
be able to prove is that I pulled you into light and begged you to dance.

THE QUIET SAINTS

by Ryk McIntyre

This world is carried on the backs of saints, hidden amongst us,
working in secret; and never the obvious ones.

1. Jesus-at-Dawn – every morning, he's the first to walk around Boston, right alongside garbage trucks. At the same time, he sees a whole other world. He is filthy coat, a belt of rope; he's the sum of his own blood-shot ways. Armored in greasy strangles of hair, he knows his gym bag is broken and he's ugly and stinks. But his eyes are fixed past visible light. He sees nothing but his next target. He traces the same path through the streets everyday- no margin for error. Too much is at stake. Tremont to School Street, School to Congress, Congress to Milk to Washington to Winter, Winter back to Tremont. His virtue is a prayer wheel that he pounds into the pavement; he's chosen buildings for prayer-beads. People laugh at the crazy man, but none of them know. When he starts to curse, and argue with nothing, when he drops his gym bag, grabs at the nothing on his shoulders, throws it to the ground, and stomps on it until it's dead, screaming, "You can't come here! I won't let you!" he's doing it for us. "The city is safe for a little while," he thinks, gathering up things that fell from his gym bag. And then it's back to the prayer wheel, where the job is ugly, but some ugly guy's gotta do it.

2. Gloria works at the Boston Public Library. She loves books in place of all the people that have hurt her. Books never lie- books always tell you the same story, every time you ask. Books have a spine. She is comforted by categories and shelves where things fit how they ought. She moves through stacks like a gray breeze, and sometimes she is invisible to men. Hard lessons are hard to unlearn. But the Dewey Decimal System is her rock. The warm feeling of Order helps her sleep at night. Tomorrow, she will deal with books, and be comforted by geometries of knowledge. She will surround herself with the armor of History, the heady madness in Comedy; fine silk Romances- she loves language, and wishes poetry could be carved in stone around every heart that's ever been wounded by words. She still dreams of being a mother someday, imagines teaching her child to read. So she gives books to friends and strangers, daycares and detoxes, homeless shelters and elected officials. She says "God, if these words are all I'll ever know of human, let everything be an open book in my forgiving heart, a gift I truly know how to give."

3. There are people who live in the world and have no idea who they are. They think they're small, living quiet lives, certain the Universe doesn't notice. A quiet strength, they are secret pillars that hold the world up for every tomorrow. The World is moving all the time and they are spokes of the great creation wheel of its creation. They are Brazil butterflies that hurricane the shores of Heaven. They feed the walls of the world to keep them from falling in, with the mortar of their ordinary: the way Gloria re-shelves books ensures Spring follows Winter every year; and Boston would've been overrun by invisible demons since the 1980s, if it weren't for Jesus-at-Dawn chanting runes of power into the sidewalks, the whole universe shaking a little bit with his every small step.

THE TONY STARK HANDBOOK
OF FAMILIAL LOVE

by A. Bissa

1. your father is the sun.
2. watch your mother fade without him, or with him, the sun like a bell curve,
   drunk on money, power, drunk.
3. not drunk, because you don't know about that.
4. build something to love you. ask how something without a heart loves you better.
5. go away.
6. get drunk on youth, freedom, drunk.
7. convince yourself that this is how a father loves.
8. disregard conflicting evidence, like a good scientist.
9. decide pure science is bullshit, and engineering is the best, because engineering makes
   things, and, as with love, science is only really worth anything when something tangible
   comes of it.
10. poor little rich boy screws his way through eastern Massachusetts.
11. twelve days after your twenty-first birthday, you are an orphan and a billionaire.
12. poor little rich boy screws his way through a burial, a magazine cover, a college graduation,
    a corporate handover, a cross-country move, and the third decade of his life.
13. your name is Tony, and your epithet is genius, fuck-up, problem child,
    king of the world wearing a lead crown of your own construction.
14. your mother died worrying about you. the furrow in your brow looks like a
    headstone.

TEACHING MY SOUL TO FLY

by Susan Dobbe Chase

I think back to my Wonder
Woman childhood,
where bad guys
looked like skeletons,
and the good people
were the attractive ones.

Blankets thrown over bad memories.
The few shocking times
I heard grown-ups cry like children.
The dripping tap of my wonder
years keeping me up at night.

Clear morality eroding.
The bones of my arms lengthening,
The mass of my body growing,
Brain pathways snipped.
Possibility to definition.

Once I was sexless. Now I am not,

Whittled from something pure
into something pointed.
Shrunken while I became larger.
Lessons, string by string,
strapping Gulliver dreams to the ground.

I think ahead to the flying cars
of my science-fiction future
where all the bad guys look like robots
and the good people wear lab coats.

Complicated morals explored
and the few shocking times
we get things right.
The electric hum of my age
helping me sleep at night.

Predictions of the past,
naive and childish-small,
eroding further into black.

The bones of my spine shrinking,
muscles weakening.
The pathways of my brain,
snipped from hard structure
to gusts of unsuspected memory.

Now I am sexual. Soon I won't be.

Electrified from the primitive.
Parts of me replaced.
My hopes, kite by kite,
teaching my soul to fly.

ASTRO BOY BLUES

by Gary Jackson

rap your knuckles on my skin   show
me that you care   you
can't jostle my hair   you
can oil the black metal   make
it shine   clean
me up like your own ten year old boy   if
I don't love you   don't
take it personal   you're
the wrong shape   my
friends have Pythagorean angles   slice
open hands when they shake   they
say accept no substitutions   I'm
the improvement on the real McCoy   I'm
the AC on a high noon day   use
me in place of the natural breeze   I'll
keep you cool

POPEYE THE SAILOR ON LOVE

by Rob Sturma

Lisken.

I cant's tells ya nothin' ya don'ts already know.
Wimming will be the deaths of ya if ya let em be,
but theys kin also saves yer life.

I gets exasperpated when I sees perfeckly amazin' wimming
fallin' fer the same ol' manipulashkun overs and overs,
cuz they don't feels like they gotsk the right to be equalified
with their sweetie. That's a load of jeep crap.
Olives and I are equalipated in every way. We boths take care
of me Swee'Pea, we boths go shoppifying for veggigables
and cold cucks and such, we takes turns washin' dishkes.

I yam happy as Wimpy at McDonalds when we settles on the couch
and watch our shows (She likes Wheels of Forchkun, I watches
Parks and Recreeayskun).   No, we don't always agree on everthings.
But she loves me. She wraps her pipe cleaner body
around my misk-shapen forearms and and whiskerpates my name
into me cauliflower ear.   She makes me heart pitter-pat so fask
I feel dizzier then when Bluto spins me around.
When she goes away, my stomach hurts
like The Sea Hag put broken glass in me spinach.

I says to her, "Olives, I loves ya. And I wishes
I could be hooked up to a spinach IV
so's I could saves ya twenky four hours a day."

And Olives looks at me with those raisinks for eyeballs,
and says in her prettified screech of a voice,
"Oh, Popeye. I don't WANT to be saved all the time.
Sometimes I just want to be sad or scared or in distress
so I can save myself every once in a while."

And that's when the freight trains start exclatin' in me muskles
and the spinach can pops open in me chesk
and that's when I realizes, that in that momenk,
that perfeck momenk,
our loves is strong to the finnich.

And in that momenk,
I yam saved too.

THE REAL DARK KNIGHT

by Lindsay King-Miller

why so serious?

you played it so straight
we could smell you.
such glee in the way things were broken
who could believe it was a lie
you joker. you bleeding smile.

you played that wild card for keeps.
swallowed it whole and it spit you out
limping and invincible.
when you died every pilot light
in the city of gotham wept
flammable tears.

your final role will be the marrow
of legends, you saw-toothed magician,
you myth. you are paper and ink
and infamy all longer-lived than flesh
as long as men can breathe
and be afraid.

we will remember you
with makeup flaking. dirty hair.
no one will know if you had scars
for real. when you were alive
you laughed like a ghost
and no one will ever play it
as raw as you did.

decades from now there will be scholars
in the way you lick your lips.
we will remember you
as a brilliant enemy
you died undefeated
blazing with gorgeous ugliness.

you died sweating nitroglycerine.
your coffin was lined with lead.
we believe you will scratch
your way back with tenacity
and dynamite we believe
we can't get rid of you so easily.

I hope you know
you will be remembered this way
forever, you clown, you madman
we will write on your grave
in lipstick we will carve
a eulogy into flesh we will make you
fight for an honest obituary.

did you die knowing you were immortal
tell me, you joker, seriously
what's it like to last beyond
your final chapter?

we will always be writing your name
in gasoline on the skyline
you razor in the mouth of predictability.
you are watching the city burn.
you are licking the smoke from your lips
God you used to have lips
you are dancing in ashes
you are ashes.

I hope they buried you in a purple suit
you agent of chaos.
you russian roulette coin eater
motherfucker you conjurer
endlessly swallowing snakes
napalm tongue trickster god
you joker.

you were ugly when you died.
you were laughing.
and we who will remember that laugh
forever have already
forgotten your name.

OPEN LETTER TO BATMAN, FROM ROBIN

by David Ayllon

Today I was bit by a stray pit bull
and I thought of your kiss.

My boyfriend was surprised
to come home and find
I had stitched up the wound
with thread
and bare teeth.

Batman, I've grown up.

He doesn't know about you, about
how small my hands were in yours.
It was always so hard to tell the difference
between the watercolor bruises I gave you
and the ones they did.

When I asked if we could get a bird,
you'd point to some caged criminal
and say, "Here.
Here is your bird."
Because nothing says love
like a fallen enemy; a bouquet
of artery and tendon.

You were such a reluctant brute, skin
painted tight onto muscle.

I used to wander into empty phone booths
looking for a boy with Superman's chin
and Clark Kent eyes. The kind of hero
who knows which side is his good side;
who would never hide his face.

But I found you.

I've always known a little something
about secrets. About alter-egos.
About lives split right down the spine.
About hoping they'll believe you
when you show them a mask and call it your face.

When I try to understand
what made us do what we did

I come up with a different answer every time.
Because we will always be creatures of excess,
because "don't ask, don't tell" does not exist for a vigilante,
because what we did needed to be big enough to overshadow
what we were.

Our secrets were orphaned dreams,
and we held them like young grenades.
So we fashioned our hearts into phalanx;
put on the cloak
and the dagger.
An army of lovers, the two of us.

It was unnatural how your arms
were both weapon and valentine; how
your shoulder blade doubled as home.
You said these are the skills of the outcast

and I'm just now beginning to understand
that sometimes there is more peril
in holding another man's hand
than breaking it;
Our costumes were merely dressing the wound.
We used the spotlight as veneer,
violence as disguise.
We did everything we thought made a man just that.

This is why I hate Halloween, Bruce.
Why I left that city.
I saw you in every one of its frown lines.

You chose Gotham over me.
You chose Batman.

And while you may caress the skyline,
I have courage enough to steal
a kiss from my lover down on the street.

You said I cut off my own wings,
But, Bruce, I can wear his hands.
Just like a cape.

SHOESHINE BOY FINDS JESUS

by Kathleen Delaney-Adams

In a dog eat dog world,
no one prays for the underdog.
No one, that is, but an anthropomorphic canine TV reporter named Jesus.
Jesus appeared to me in a phone booth one quiet morn,
to illustrate for me the crimes and sins
committed by those who have not chosen to follow His path,
the path of the righteous and meek.

As His chosen, the meekest of the meek,
a mere Shoeshine Boy,
I was given a ring, the ring of God,
whose secret compartment was filled
with the answer to all our fears.
One teeny pill,
and I was transcended from earthly form
into a doglike personification of Superman.

In the land of good vs. evil
the villains must be stopped,
and Jesus has shown me the way to
Virtuous Super Powers --
Drugs.
Once thought the way to damnation,
the Drugs of Jesus will lead us to righteousness.
My great calculating brain evolved through prayer and hallucinogenics.
And here is my prayer:
"Without my Super Energy Pill
(Given to me by His Lord, my personal Savior)
I grow weaker and weaker and weaker still."

Through prayer, Cosmic Ray Vision, and drugs,
I am able to abdicate evil demons from the world
and thus spread the Word of The Lord.
The meek shall indeed inherit
and Shoeshine Boy prevails,
Flying beyond supersonic speeds,
moving entire planets out of harm's way,
and quoting the Testament in rhyme:

"The Lord is my Shepherd, I shall not want.
He maketh me to lie down in green pastures,
He leadeth me beside the still waters,
He giveth me Self-Propelled Flight to flaunt.
Amen."

LARGER THAN LIFE

by David Ohlsen

3. When I was ten, I had this dream about wrestling.
I was in the center of the ring
and the crowd was going wild.
They chanted my name
and their voices echoed
like a million tunnels of color.
I lifted a man
larger than the sky
above my head
and held him there
while he quaked, squirmed,
& prayed to disappear.

4. By eighteen I was living above a boxing gym.
My parents had thrown me out a year before
for coming home after losing my first light heavyweight match
and cutting the couch in half
with a crowbar and some hedge clippers.
I was shooting trenbolone acetate every day
and selling it to the freshmen.
Guys around the gym got to calling me "Bug"
'cause I could bench twice my own body weight
but my eyes would bulge out every time.
I swept up the place, kept the bathrooms clean,
answered all the phones as best as I could,
and then I messed up~

forgot to lock up one night
after setting a new record on the leg press,
and the addicts got in.
Stole the TVs, stole the register,
broke into the vending machines
and pissed on the mats.
The owner kicked me out.
I used the last of the TB
in a Ralph's bathroom,
beat up the first dope fiend I found
wandering around
the recycling center in the parking lot,
then went to my dealer's house
to find something new.

5. By the time I was twenty-three
I'd blown through all of my best options
on the modern drug market.
PCP made me feel invincible,
like an illuminated character in a video game,
but I usually woke up in jail or in the hospital.
I met a girl with blue eyes, bleached hair,
black nail polish and an Adderall prescription
and for a while, that was nice- that was enough.
Every other day we'd wander to another pharmacy,
flirt with the white coats
and try on cheap sunglasses.
Then I pushed it too far, like I always do-
a few extra pills
a few extra shots
a few extra lines
a few extra hits-
and when I woke up in the crash house the next morning,
she didn't.
No one did.
We all knew the coke was bad
and we did it anyway.
I wiped away the blood from her nose & mouth
with a Star Wars bed sheet.
I tried to find her pulse, but she was so cold.
I tried to find my own,
and I was cold, too.
I wasn't breathing. I was ice.
I freaked & grabbed the nearest half-empty syringe
and pushed it into me
without even looking for a vein,
but felt nothing.
I covered my gums with the bad coke,
but felt nothing.
I hadn't woken up that sober
since sophomore year
and it was worse than
waking up dead.
My arachnid skin grew colder by the second
and my eyes opened wider to view
the nightmares of unaltered reality~
how clearly one can separate
shadows from the sun.
Vodka tasted like air, I couldn't swallow,
smoke was elusive
without working lungs.
I could no longer impatiently farm
the gratifications of sensuality.

Looking at myself in the mirror,
I saw a pigeon shit covered, turquoise statue
of Frankenstein's monster-
orphaned by science
and free from the mechanics
of God's mercy.

6. The father of Jerry Siegel,
the man who invented Superman,
died when gangsters attempted to rob
the clothing store he owned
in New York's Lower East Side.
In Jerry's helplessness, he invented an alien
that could solve problems he couldn't.
He created an alternate universe
that housed a single different being
with a different set of rules;
a being that could overcome
the boundaries of mortality.
Jerry knew what had to be done.
He knew that anger
and fear
couldn't be the final words.
He knew how deeply we all hope
to be something more.

7. I always wanted to be big & strong.
A Hulk. A Beast.
A man larger than life.
A giant hidden
between lost dimensions.
Big always wins, always,
so, big never has to be afraid.

8. I like to perch along Golden Gate Bridge
or on a tall branch in Aokigahara forest
and listen for those lonely, one-way footsteps.
I follow them
and I whisper,
and as I rot away
I ask them to tell me
about their dreams.

BIZARRO HATE POEM

by Jesse Parent

Good-bye Lois.

Me hate you.
Me hate you more than kittens.
Let me explain.
Kittens killed me mother.
They rolled giant boulder of yarn over cliff onto Bizarro Mommy.
Bizarro Mommy scream, "Yeeeeeessssss!"
as boulder of yarn crushed her angled face into smooth, beautiful curves.
We closed casket because of all the vomiting.

Me hate you like dew on morning flower.
Let me explain.
Moisture causes explosive reaction with pure sodium.
Me put pure sodium on everything.
French fries.
Fried eggs.
Infant cousin.
Me little cousin burned in her small crib to a blackened crisp.
Me laugh and laugh and laugh when me remember.
Me can still taste the smoke, salty and thick.
Me think of this when me lie in bed in dark Bizarro house,
when wood floor creaks like tiny shrieking.
Me never sleep without drinking whole pint of grain alcohol.

Me hate you like sunrise.
Let me explain.
Sunrises are cloud poop.
Molten cloud poop.
Hot molten cloud poop that burn cloud butt hole.
Me wish you were cloud.

Me want to throw you into side of mountain.
Me want to fly you into deepest ocean trench and let go.
Me make contribution in your name to Tea Party and give them all of your phone
    numbers,
so they call you at inconvenient times, day after day.
They always need more money.
It ok.
On Bizarro World, they really good people.

That how much me hate you.
Like sunrise.
Like morning dew.
Like kittens.
Like mountainsides.
Like deepest oceans.
Like Tea Party.

Will you divorce me?

EIGHT ARMS TO HOLD YOU

by Jeff Austin

A single bare bulb hung over the workbench as Peter continued his tireless pace, just like he had for the last two months. Or was it three? Whatever the case, he was going to make sure the whole school knew his name and his face for something else besides a punchline and a punching bag.

It started with the field trip to the science museum. The students milled around but Harry and Peter were standing in front of the gamma radiation exhibit together, Peter taking in the complex machine with its display of the powerful energy while Harry talked about his father with a combination of disdain and admiration.

Neither of the boys noticed a single spider had rappelled down into the path of the beam that danced between the two posts and was now crawling up the railing in front of them. Now they were talking face-to-face, Peter's body turned towards the machine while Harry was leaning back on his hands against the railing.

Harry yanked his hand away from the rail with a pained grimace and a few quick expletives. Peter recognized it as a spider bite and first aid was applied. Fast forward a couple of weeks later, the entire city was buzzing about this Spider-Man fellow, with Peter being the only one to figure out who he actually was while everyone at school (including Mary Jane)swooned over the masked wall-crawler.

Peter finished up and slipped the device on, placing the controls around his head. The two pair of automated tentacles that ran out of the pack on his back writhed in tune with his thoughts, moving mechanically and effortlessly with every impulse. Harry might have had looks, money, and now superpowers but Peter had brains and a huge chip on his shoulder.

SQUIRREL GIRL: THE PLAYBOY INTERVIEW

by Wonder Dave

after Laura Yes Yes

A: Yes, I can in fact talk to squirrels.

A: Squirrels have a much more sophisticated culture
   than most humans would expect.

A: Yes, my tail is prehensile.

A: No, I wouldn't.

A: Logan has always been prone to melodramatic fits.

A: You've blurred the line there, buddy boy.

A: I don't need luck. I eat nuts.

A: I've always thought my buck teeth were cute.

A: Hazelnuts, at least that's what the boys say.

A: I have low light vision so that's a bonus.

A: Steve Ditko and Will Murray obviously. I am also a big fan of Dan Slott.

A: It was not a Doom-Bot. Everyone in the capes and tights game knows it.

A: I once autographed a pair of Squirrel Girl Underoos for a Deadpool cosplayer,
while he was wearing them.

A: Ever since I was a little squirrel.

A: I got the best job in the world. I'm a hero.

NO FOOLIN'

by Stephen Meads

There is never a point at which the Joker goes too far and Batman snaps
his neck and that's the end of it, no more random blown up things
no more hundreds of babies abducted and killed, no more grins
spread too wide across faces that cannot bear it and split
lips hideously open and laughing, no more sidekicks beaten
to death with a crowbar. (That last one was so funny though
because all the fans cheered the Joker on in his destruction;
they were in on it). Watching Batman open up his heart to this punk
kid that really didn't deserve it, only to see him turned to bruise
all pointalized purple and red, swollen lips not giving into the joke
just holding on for his death to come. In some ways it was an attack
on Batman's own heart, beaten again and again; the Dark Knight never snaps.
He never breaks down, gives over to insanity, lips peeling up
at the corners in the kind of grin that will kill you;
he is never a gun going "bang", because he cannot be a gun.
He is only and always a man, and his heart is always that thing
breaking in the night like the worst belly laughter,
and his eyes are always that dark bruise purpling to hell,
and this joke, that because he is a man he will always lose
everything he loves, because that is the point of men
to go so far past babies and smiles and blown up distortions of life
and not lose it, is something that the Joker will never get;
he will never go far enough.

THE HISTORY OF BRAILLE (OR ELEKTRA'S LAST LETTER TO MATT MURDOCK)

by Jennifer Leigh-Oprihory

I.

Once upon a time, there were men who punched stars into parchment
in the name of giving soldiers
the ability to speak without light
and called it night writing,

but a blind boy stole it
and manipulated it so that the world
could fit beneath the tip of his finger —
a 2x3 dot-matrix theory of everything —
and added music so that the words wouldn't have to live alone.

Then the dots took his name.

He wasn't trying to save the world.
He just set out to make sense of the darkness.
The rest is history.

II.

If you were paper,
then braille would be a language of scars
decipherable only by the blind
designed to be freed by touch.

III.

I spoke scar
before πατέρας
before English
before America
before therapy
before Columbia
before Chaste
before *assassin*
before you.

IV.

Matt, if I'd written a proper letter
Bullseye would've folded it into
an aerodynamic death wish
an origami contract
to cement his ties to Kingpin

so I printed everything I could never say
into my skin.

I wanted to be an open book for you
so that you could remember me
as something more than a scarlet trail
and a flash mob.

V.

We can't all be heroes.

We can't all walk quietly
carrying big sticks to save us.

Sometimes it takes a sword.

Sometimes, the sword takes us.

VI.

We can't all be heroes,
but we can always be paper.

VII.

This is my body: Read from it.

I am your braille.

THE FLASH CRASHES MY FATHER'S SECOND WEDDING

by Kieran Collier

The day the Flash decided to crash my father's second wedding
nobody tried to stop him. I asked for his autograph,

my younger cousins challenged him to a race, and my sister
flirted with him while he vibrated through the ice sculpture of Cupid.

He said he didn't believe in fake gods, then laughed
while tossing back a glass of champagne. After the I Do's,

I asked him why the ice sculpture didn't melt as he passed through it,
because vibrating molecules are supposed to create heat.

He told me that the speed force was a funny thing—it exists
so we can break through it, but we can't truly understand it.

I asked why he was there in the first place. He said he crashes
weddings all the time, unexpectedly saving what could have been

a potentially boring ceremony. I asked why he let my cousins
beat him in a race. He said that sometimes he likes to be

someone else's favorite, at least for a little while. I asked why
he always had an answer to my questions. He asked why I always

had to question his answers, why I was asking
questions in the first place. So I asked him the question

that had been on my mind the entire time: could my dad
love his new wife the same way he loved his old one?

The Flash tells me that the speed force is a funny thing,
that it exists so that we can break through it. He tells me grief
is the same way. That we must acknowledge that it is always
around us, but that the only way to move is to go on
not in spite, but because of the losses we have already had.

He tells me that love
is a funny thing, but he's sure if my mom
was looking down she would love
that my father has learned to love again.

SUPERVILLAIN

by The Klute

I never wanted to be a superhero
On the playground,
When the other boys were scaling the jungle gym as Spiderman
Or running around with makeshift capes
Fashioned from plastic lunchroom tablecloths
I would be alone in the sandbox…
Plotting.

Fuck Superheroes!

My role models were Lex Luthor, the Joker, Black Manta
Like them I wanted the world to accept me on my own terms.
And I wanted an army of laser wielding spider robots!
I… am The Klute.
A member of the Legion of Doom and the Guild of Calamitous Intent
I've got mad scientists on speed dial
A closest full of doomsday devices,
And unlike God, I DO play dice with the Universe.
20-sided dice.

I never understood how they sell people on the Superman trip?
"So, let me get this straight –
I get to risk my life – for free – saving the world from certain death,
And then I get to go work at a dead-end desk job
Where at the end of the day my girlfriend's gone, my family's dead,
And my friends… are also dead?"
No thank you.
The flipside however, supervillainy, is a pretty sweet gig.
You get neat gadgets, like the psychofrakulator
Or the previously mentioned laser-wielding spider robots.
Instead of a lame catchphrase like "Shazam!" or "Up, Up, and Away!"
You get an evil laugh that's accentuated with big, bold capital letters that always go off panel!
HAHAHAHAHAHA!

Your costume isn't some homoerotic pastel one-piece
It's probably black with a majestic sweep
Or a classic suit with a nice trim
As a supervillain, you get henchmen with metal teeth
Instead of sidekicks with abandonment issues
Your girlfriend isn't the prim-and-proper Lois Lane or Mary-Jane
Who'll only put out when you're in costume.
As a supervillain, you'll get women who appreciate the sensitive soul behind the metal mask and 40-foot

Reed Richards was a dorky scientist,
Victor Von Doom a rich socialite.
Peter Parker, the nerdy loser
Harry Osborn the popular kid.
Anyone else sensing a pattern here?

Plus, you've got focus –
You're not trying to discover the truth behind your mysterious origins
While bringing your parent's killers to justice
And trying to fit in to a hostile world.
No for the supervillain it's:
Step One: Take over the world
Step Two: Enjoy!
Best of all, the other guy's bound by the rules… BUT YOU'RE NOT!
Captain Sunshine can't send Wonder Boy off to die to cover his escape…
But I can.
In fact all of you are just pawns in my plans for world domination,
And I have to sacrifice you to see those plans come to fruition
Well, that's just one less mouth to feed in the new world order

And I'm cool with that, because I'm a supervillain.
I always wanted to be one.
I would laugh when the Spiderman wannabe fell from the jungle gym to the concrete jungle
below
Or when little Jimmy's plastic lunchroom cape would snag on a door
And drop him like Kryptonite
But I wouldn't laugh because I was evil
(well, maybe a tad)
I just knew that from the security of my sandbox sanctum
That they were suffering the inevitable fate of every superhero
They were chumps – ready to take the fall
Suckers – for living up to the expectations everyone had for them.
Fools. FOOLS!!!
And I'll show them! I'll show them all!

THE SPIDER-MAN

by Zachary Kluckman

My name is Spider-man. Or it should have been.

The moon is a spider's egg; a hollow silk tube birthing a thousand small bodies on silver
    safety lines,
falling through the dark to crawl inside our mouths while we sleep.

The moon invades our bodies this way. A birth-tide of arachnids,
our pulse alive with their movements.

When they touch me, uncle, I think of you,
how my body hung from your web; how I bit my knuckles until they bled,
how the bone broke the flesh, egg sacks hidden in my fists,

the skin crawls across my chest remembering trap doors.
Webs strung between my shoulders, waiting to catch your thumbs
twisted ugly as the dried husks of spiders spilled across my body.

I wish I had been as lucky as them. Born near blind despite the number of eyes
so I had not been forced to watch the things you did to me.

You studied their bodies almost as closely as mine. Admired the divine
physiology of eight legged machines designed for survival. Pages torn from field guides
hung from every wall, blueprints of their bodies that taught me to recognize
the genus, family and species of every horror you set loose on my six year old chest.

You forced me to my knees to worship at the altars of torture with your hot, moist breath in
my ears.

Don't move. They're more afraid of you
than you are of them.

Your fingernails like knives as they crawled in my mouth, small dead things on my tongue.
The stiff dark hair of your fingers an iron brush across my stomach.
Your hands were bigger than my head, but you let the spiders touch me first.

You didn't have the nerve to be the first one across my body,
already afraid of the hero I would become.

My name is Zachary, but you can call me Spider-man, uncle;
because I learned how to scream from the spiders, to thrash my legs in the air, to crawl
and hide behind chairs, eyes blackened with fear.

In a world where spiders are as common as colds,
you left me to grow up afraid of what I would become.
To question every relationship, fear every touch, hide from every hand.

With great power comes great responsibility, uncle. You betrayed yours.
When my children were born I was afraid to hold them.
Afraid the spiders would come.

An arachnid fascination with web building, trapping small bodies in cocoons of bed sheets
and secrets, you almost stole my faith in love.
I had to learn the truth from comic books: that heroes have to save themselves first.

You tried to convince me some stories could never be told, because it's unfair to ask
anyone to hear them. If there's any power in names, then there is power in naming our
demons.
So this one is for you,
Stephen.

The moon is an egg sac hung high in the corner of the sky. I still have trouble going outside
alone in the evening and I am still afraid of spiders,

but I survived you. I saved myself, and even if the scars you left make me ugly,
I love without wearing a mask.

THE DRY CLEANER

by John F. Buckley and Martin Ott

The Ten-Second Martinizer? A valuable ally. And Tetrachloroethylene Lad's sacrifice
will never be forgotten. But the number-one living superhuman dry cleaner remains
Randolph. He once had a last name, but the solvents have stripped away the wrapping.

If your cape retains its bounce in mid-flight and is able to withstand mildew, sonic booms
and tumbles with villains and coin-operated dryers, you likely owe this cleaner your life.
He began as a sidekick for The Mad Tailor, keeping his needles and thread garrote sharp.

Now he lurks in his lair there on Excelsior and Wayne, a plate-glass affair hiding soap turrets,
hot-air bazookas, and, for demonic possession of synthetic fabrics, a sanctified Kremble of
Eighth-Level Wodd. Randolph had thumb-wrestled The Blot of Andromeda

and steam cleaned the tag team of Scourge and Dirge, pre-apocalyptic poetic bards
whose dirty limericks and obituary-inspired verse caused bloomers to rise and hearts to
burst. His friends and lovers occasionally rankled at the need for a ticket to see him,

at the black linen domino mask that fooled no one, but made Randolph feel, he said,
"one with the cause." Yet they forgave him, for his modesty, for his aversion to cheap
wire hangers, for the cosmic oath of commitment to cleaning he intoned each morning.

The world was a dirty place and he knew his role in it, rubbing out alien armadas
and grass stains in knees with equal aplomb, with a passion boiling over from tight
bulletproof undergarments and the resolve to roil the earth on a gentle spin cycle.

THE CAPE AND COWL CAN'T HIDE MY DISAPPOINTMENT

by Alan Passman

Maxime,
the Parisian dandy of the Halloween party,
offered you a seat

and you sat on that fucking frog's lap
as he posed there in a goddamned deck chair,
from his cherry lips spouted heavy tongued bullshit.

"Comb on, Comb on…
Jus juan quiche,
jus juan quiche,
jus juan…"

Holding his hand up,
finger outstretched to symbolize the number
he butchered the pronunciation of.
You playfully smiled, smoking a cig like a big girl,
that same smile you shoot me from time to time
wearing those Bardot-style, mocha knee highs

like now

walking right on by, perhaps because it was dark,
perhaps because I was dressed as Batman,
blending with the night, like him,
brooding, like him.

FRUSTRATION: THE GOSPEL OF LEX LUTHOR

by Hannibal Tabu

I first split the atom when I was twelve years old.

While waiting for my high school diploma,
I proved the Hodge conjecture
and devised my first weapon of mass destruction.

I've devised profitable patents
while waiting for microwave popcorn.

Decades since I sat in a barber's chair.
My best friends are pathological psychopaths.
Instead of being lauded as the finest mind
humanity has ever developed,
I'm considered a criminal
a deviant
a villain.

My twelve-year-old mind found it all so simple.
Never having access to Oppenheimer's notes,
red hair still waiting to be born
underneath my pasty chest.
Complicated mathematic equations
like music in my mind,
I hummed as I wrote them out,
sang aloud as I contained the reaction
that powered the lab I hid in the gardener's shed
for the next two years.

Without the shadow of that ... invader
fluttering over my head
I could be anything.
President wasn't big enough,
standing astride worlds of finance and commerce
took less focus than urinating.
My intellect could administrate galaxies,
power contained in my all-too-human mind meat
could follow the paths of six thousand gamma waves
across seven parsecs
while making myself a sandwich
and solving world hunger.

But I can't.
Can't concentrate on curing cancer
or solving any Rubik's Cube in fourteen moves.
Can't sit down to write
all four symphonies I've had in my head
since the night I lost my virginity.

All I can do is look up in the sky
and dream about the day
I'll bring it down to earth.

BRUCE WAYNE WAKES UP

by Mark Palos

I wake up, 10:32am. It's a cold morning in Gotham. I know this before I get out of bed.

Every broken bone, every bullet that failed its intended purpose, every time someone struck
my shadow-self in fear or anger -- predicts the weather for me.

It's been nineteen years since I found my answer;
thirty-five since I was born again, in an alley.
I've lost count of the nights, given up on ever having anything else.

Without a sound, somehow, Alfred knows I'm awake, enters the room.
Places my breakfast:
An apple,
two pieces of dry wheat toast,
and a protein shake
on the nightstand.
Throws open the curtains.
We don't talk.

I place my feet on the floor. He paws at me like a teenage boy on a first date. Surveys the
bruises. Raises each of my arms, leans over and checks the bandage, the stab wound he
stitched up two mornings ago. Just as silently, he exits the room, satisfied that I don't need
medical attention for once.

I take the apple from the tray, step to the window. The night's rain still clings to the glass.
At this hour, the city looks more alive than I feel. I take a bite of the apple. Two of my
teeth are loose.

I fill the bathroom sink with warm water, submerge my hands, get them to a point where I
can move my fingers without visibly wincing.

I run on the treadmill. Stare out of the window.
Recite the names of every victim who I could have
but failed
to save.

I don't stop running until I name them all.
It takes about 45 minutes these days.

The last two are always my parents.

I shower and dress for the noon meeting with Lucius. He's retiring next year. Keeps telling
me that he'll worry about me. Keeps asking me to promise I'll call him if I need anything.

I straighten my tie in my mother's mirror. Put my father's fountain pen in my inside pocket.

I look at my own reflection: 44 years old,
Two years older than my father, when he choked out his last words,
Bruce… don't be afraid.

The last thing I put on before I leave for the day is the watch she gave me. 14 years ago.
It was my birthday. A cheap thing, but inscribed, it says,
You are loved for who you are,
Not what you do,
Remember this,
In the darkest parts of the night.

I looked into her eyes, told her that I loved her, that she would never have to be afraid.

I will never see her again.

I can't bring her back.

I can't bring any of those names back.

My punishment for this failure is that I will die alone. Maybe in an alley, maybe in a bed, but
that doesn't mean I won't step in the way of every bullet from now until my moment comes.

Their sum might equal all the parts where I fell short.
Might find me some measure of peace.

No one will ever know that I think of her each morning. I think Alfred suspects, because I
never speak of her. But he knows not to ask.

I will never see her again, and I hope that when my moment comes, I will die making sure
that some stranger never has to feel the way I feel…
every morning.

PUNY HUMAN

by Doc Luben

On the TV show his name was David.
I remember, 'cause that was MY name.
To a five year old
that is a big deal.
TV bosses thought the name "Bruce" was too feminine.
So we also had that in common.

When his transformations started,
when his eyes flashed blue into green and
I knew the snarling visage of Lou Ferrigno
would soon rage onto the screen,
I would leap behind the sofa,
watching between the cushions,
eyes huge with the fear
of recognition.

I practiced roaring.
I made walls from cardboard boxes so I could smash through them.
I was grounded twice
for scissor cutting muscle rips into my shirts.
I even tried to learn how to run in slow motion.

THE HULK, like all heroes, has a hundred origins,
but the primal details stay the same:
a blast of gamma radiation,
a foolish and impulsive act of heroism,
Bruce Banner,
caught in a shockwave of green fire,
his body metamorphosed into a waking nightmare,
his spirit torn into halves.
Most of the time, he just looks normal.
It's only sometimes
            that he gets
                    the other way.

My transformations
did not start until I was older.
My origin had no cinematic explosions.
I was six days old. I choked on milk.
My face turned blue (not green).
The icy Rochester roads kept us from the hospital.
Asphyxiation leads to aneurysm.
An adorable infant aneurysm.

I survived, of course,
with just a small knot of scar tissue
nestled in the center of my brain.
They call it "a shadow"
a dark black mark on the MRI.
It irritates the surrounding tissue,
but the neurons only spike a little bit.
Most of the time.

Most of the time
I am fine. Normal.
Most of the time
I am me.

The textbook name is
Complex Partial Frontal Lobe Seizure.
A name good enough for science fiction.
In fact, when it happens, this is true:
doctors call it "an episode."

I am lucky. I would never dare say otherwise.
My shadow has never gotten bigger.
The kind of seizure I get
does not reach my body.
It just makes me

confused.
I forget how long
I have been standing still
with my hand on a box of cereal.
I hear echoes that are not there.
I hear knocking, like someone inside the wall.
Sometimes, my name being whispered
from somewhere behind me.
Not the name I go by now.
My old name.
My childhood name. David.

Sometimes I talk in machine gun bursts
        that I can't stop, even when someone
at the bus stop
            looks right at me, I can't stop, or

I cry,
provoked by nothing,
just cry
and cry and cry so hard I can't breathe
and I sit on the front porch and scratch at my knuckles

and pray for everyone
to quit pretending they love me
so I could kill myself without it being
some big fucking deal.

Then I say things like that.
Things that make people scared.
Things I cannot take back.

This other person lives inside of me.
And he is big. And he is mean.
And he is stronger than I am.
He doesn't give me time to explain.
He arrives in a slow wave of green fire,
not without warning--- without warning would be better---
but with a hiss pulse countdown from thirty,
enough to hear him coming,
with no way to stop him.
I can't warn bystanders. I can't tell it fast enough.
The exposition doesn't all fit in one panel.
My body doesn't change.
My disease is not the kind you can see.
speech bubble
I am sorry I didn't mean to say that.
No, I can't just calm down.
I am not upset, I am on fire.
I can't just breathe deep think positive.
I didn't mean what I said. I didn't say what I said.
That person you were talking to wasn't me.

I live like Bruce Banner. I stay close to the exit.
I am always listening
for that low growl
that starts in the bone behind my ears,
and when I hear it
I don't wait to see what's going to happen.
I put as much goddamn distance as I can
between me and anyone
who I could hurt.
Just leave the party without saying goodbye.
Text your friend later
and pretend you didn't see them.
I do not ask for help.
The nightmare scenario
is anyone trying to help.

Better off, just don't go to the party.
It's better to be thought of as a flake than a monster.
Cancel that promising first date
before it begins.
Cancel that promising fourth date
                before they find out who is in here.

There is no hero hidden in the noise.
No weeping rambling bulletproof titan.
This is the thing I can do.
This is the one thing I can do for you.
I can run.
I promise I won't make a scene.
I know how to run in slow motion.

This is the best thing about being a kid
whose favorite superhero is The Hulk.
You don't have get anyone to play with you.
You can play Hulk by just going through your day
trying to keep anyone
from noticing you are there.

INTANGIBLE

by Eric Morago

I.

At twelve years old I was in love with a girl
I could never touch.

Kitty Pryde was everything
a nerdy preteen dreams of—
next-door-sweetheart-sexy,
a computer whiz, and (my mother
would have been so proud) Jewish.

She was also a ninja with a pet purple
dragon. I'd picture the loyal beast,
perched, guarding over our bicycles
outside the arcade where we'd spend
quarters as if they were kisses—
as if we would never run out.

Most importantly, she was an X-Man.
A mutant. Born different. An outcast.
What misshapen, near-sighted, metal-mouthed
twelve-year-old boy wouldn't fall for her kind
of special? Her power, to phase through walls

(and my heart), to walk through anything—
be a ghost, float on air, untouchable.
I thought, *how astonishing, such freedom.*

II.

Thirty-three and I've learned to love women
of flesh, not fiction—

have found romance beyond the splash
pages of comic books, and understand
how the real thing is much better than
any twelve-year-old boy can imagine.

(Though I still wish for a pet purple dragon.)

I know now how necessary the tactile is—
skin to skin like rain to earth,
heart to heart like bones to body.

III.

My love, now, is as much the sharp hard
glass of a mirror as she is the smoke—

Our bodies can bind to the other
the way concrete gives release
to roots' push, and yet at times,
my hand passes right through
the illusion of her presence—

as if the molecules of her heart
have acquired the talent to phase
on command when put in danger.

As we grow in this relationship,
as conversations turn to last name
changes and children, I feel she is

becoming more intangible.

I saw her the other day, fading
into an apparition, weightless,
walking a tightrope of air,
a foot off the ground, before
vanishing into the wall.

There is no freedom in this.

And I wish, more than anything,
I was twelve again, easily astonished,
perfectly content loving that which

I could never touch.

TANK GIRL DISPATCH

by Karen Garrabrant

I am still out here, but the drones
make it more difficult to be off grid
in the desert, wide open
so sometimes I live in a Hummer
retreat into a deep fur of trees.
Particularly rough times
send me into thickets of skyscrapers
and refuge under concrete ground.

Crow's feet claw at the corners of my eyes
the sun set on me, the years of living
on beer, cigarettes and sex
rounded me out, leathering my skin.
More woman now,
I am still rough kneed, big booted and sneering
fueled more by coffee and biodiesel
than fumes and adrenaline.

You can find me in gorilla girls who
score finds from trash amnesty
hack signals from discarded laptops
tinker and weld in suburban woodsheds
grease fingernails under rusted hoods in trailer parks.

As long as
the apocalyptic conditions of survival
continue, some of us
will wield glory from junk and salvage yards
like mothers make banquets
from kitchen pantries.

The clank of us
in every make, model and size
are ready with our prized calluses
when water becomes
the next fossil fuel crisis.

There is, indeed
an army of me
in motion, in periphery
always
one with the sand, the grit the dirt,
the wind carries.

MULTIPLE MAN ON CHRISTMAS EVE

by Ben Trigg

He splits up to save time.
In his typically irresponsible fashion
he has waited until the last minute to do his shopping.
He's left one of himself driving around the parking lot
searching for a space while sending an army to canvas the mall.
Coordinating from the food court, Jamie wonders what's wrong with him.
The man who can be everywhere is afraid of planning,
scared of what he'll miss if he thinks about the future.
He finds himself dangerously close to meaningful introspection,
so he turns his thoughts to his shopping list:
diamonds for Monet, a crucifix for Rahne,
Gladiator on Blu-ray for Shatterstar.
He's decided on cash for Layla. He can't surprise her anyway.
Just before midnight he leads a conga line of
gift-laden dupes down the center of the mall.
Everyone expects him to be the clown.
He might as well act like it.

FROM ONE DETECTIVE TO ANOTHER

by Kim Marshall

In search of your questions, was being faceless
something you were used to?
Gotham -- its heroes living past midnight,
always past,
you forgot how to sleep.
Dreaming was another wasted life.

In Gotham, you learned to live
in a city with nightmares. Faceless,
they emerged from their own shadows. In sleep,
the long stretch of them hid heroes, too
countless to remember. Past
midnight,

there was still more midnight,
a shadow, grave cold and silent, another life
you'd failed to save. You passed
into the same faceless
legacy, too
blank behind your mask. I know you weren't sleeping.

You didn't have time to sleep
when monsters were no longer waiting for midnight,
swarming too
many, spilling our lives
into the open. Faceless
became a new identity. It allowed me to pass --

(and what was I trying to pass
as?). You'd always been bold, slept
curved, fighting, kissing me faceless,
from Batman's shadow, our masks suspended midnight's
mirror. My life,
maybe, was the problem. I waited for my losses to

teach me: never let go of the weight. To
choose the question, did you have to pass,
wear another life
as a mask? Is this how you slept,
in the midnight shadow
of someone else's legacy, meant to be forever faceless?

You are a question they want to ignore. Even faceless,
you refused to pass, so they couldn't forget that beneath the shadow
of a man, you were not living his life. Renee Montoya is how you slept.

VILLAINS

by Robbi Ramirez

Mary,
I don't know if they read these,
so I won't pretend I'm going to
try to break you out of there.
You're a strong girl yourself,
so if your appeal does fall through
I'm sure you'll find a way, like you
always seem to do eventually.

I have a thing to do upstate, out
in the Adirondack mountains, I
can't talk too much about it yet.

When you're out of there, we won't
have to carry on like this anymore.
I know they all say that, every
bank robber and drug dealer,
but I never deluded myself. I didn't
think I had any reason to stop.
No jail can hold me, no force
can capture me alive, I can be
whatever I need to be, from air
to water to concrete to steel.

The first time I fought Thor, I
touched the head of his hammer
and became the metal of gods.
I've taken punches that could
shatter people into pink clouds
by becoming the dirt under my feet.
The first time I became water,
it took weeks to come back.
They thought they had me good,
thought they could get one past
the big, dumb Absorbing Man.

Mary. Titania. I do love you, I have
since we met at the bar. You
were wearing Doc Martens boots
and a short red dress, like you were
stalking a cocktail party looking for
a head to introduce to the curb.
But when I tell you we're done,
I don't mean "after this last job."

I know you have grudges, I do too.
But denying yourself a real life
isn't payback, that's obsession.
If you want to paint yourself green
and fuck dressed like She-Hulk,
I'm all for that, but you can't keep
tracking her down and picking fights
just because you were humiliated
in some fight ten years ago that
nobody but you even remembers.

I killed a guy last week. I was
stumbling drunk out of the bar
where we first met. I didn't see
his car, and by the time it came,
it didn't hit flesh. I was the asphalt
of the street I was standing on.
I can't do this anymore, Mary.

Don't write back, I won't be at
the address on the envelope.
I get the feeling I'll see you soon.
I might sound like my heart
is made of stone, but trust me,
I'm the great Absorbing Man.
My heart is whatever I want it to be.

Yours, always,
Carl

PROFESSOR XAVIER IS A JERK!

by Baruch Porras-Hernandez

Dear Diary: Professor Xavier is a jerk! He scolded me again
today for thinking of Colossus naked, in front of the entire X-Men! I told him that it was
perfectly normal for a young woman my age to be thinking thoughts like that and never
intrude in my mind again! Jeez! Can't a girl get a little privacy?

Dear Diary: When I hold my breath, I can feel the cold morning air, moving through me.
Neat!

Dear Diary: The Professor and I were talking today, he said that according to the theories of
multiple universes there is probably another dimension just like ours, with the same exact
planet, people, and history, but with no mutants, and no superheroes.
I cannot for the life of me imagine what that world must be like!

Dear Diary: I kissed Peter today. Holy Moley!! I'm floating! I'm floating! No, I'm on fire!

Dear Diary: Could not stop crying, went to the kitchen, Logan was there. Didn't have to
explain, he just held me, and I just let it all out. He kept drinking his beer, seemed annoyed,
but he never left, walked me back to my room. I felt like such a fool, such a little fool! I miss
my parents.

Dear Diary: Been too busy to write anything. Been a while since I've been to the states, too
busy to miss anybody! If Lockheed lights my furniture on fire one more time, I'm going to
have a very nice pair of purple shoes! Gotta go!

Journal Entry: My heart is broken.
I'm never going to see my best friend again.

Journal Entry: I can't stop thinking recently about that conversation I had with the Professor
so long ago, about the earth that exists without heroes. Every mutant I know, has dreamed at
one point in their lives, of not being a mutant. But none of us, I'm sure, has ever dreamed of
there not being any heroes.

Journal Entry: Whenever I look up into the sky, I try to picture him by Magneto's side and I
just weep. That's all I can do. Weep.

Journal Entry: Been a while, I left Europe. Excalibur is no more.
I have no idea what to do with my life. Is there a mutant with the power to cure depression?

Journal entry: Had that dream again, the world with no Avengers, no Spiderman, no
Fantastic Four, no X-Men, nothing. Every time there is a disaster, every time there is a
tragedy, thousands of people die. They just die, and that is it.

Journal Entry: Kissed Iceman, WTF?! How low have I fallen?! Bobby Drake, low! That's how low!! He can't make me laugh.
No matter how hard he tries, and I, find that horrifically, endearing. I'm back in the school, it's named after Jean. That is so sad.
I'm going to get gray hairs running this place.

Journal Entry: Everything in my body hurts. I cannot cry anymore. When did I stop being able to cry? Wolverine gave the worst eulogy, ever.
If I could, I would kill Cyclops myself.

Journal Entry: Fuck Firestar!

Journal Entry: No Storm to push back the tsunamis, no Wolverine to cut up some Sentinels, no Captain America to, I don't know…
…hit people with his shield? …what does he do again? I can't stop thinking about this alternate world where heroes don't exist.
At least they don't have to listen to Havok's bullcrap.

Journal Entry: I've left the school. I keep telling myself, that I did it for the new orphans from the past, but, part of me thinks I just did it, to run, from everything and I don't want to stop. We are in the middle of nowhere. I'm surrounded by some of the most dangerous, most wanted people on earth. My old best friend, um…who is no longer dead? -acts like there is no history between us.
I feel more alone than Peter must feel in that cave, by himself.

When I go on walks on my own, which is rare, I think about that earth, that could exist somewhere, with no superheroes. I tell myself that they must still have brave people, who want to do good.
I tell myself, that they have heroes. I tell myself that they get up every day, even when their hearts break, even when their very souls break. When they feel like nothing is ever going to get better, like us, they get up, fight just as hard, but without superpowers and because of that, my heart gets full of so much hope, it hurts.

Then I hold my breath and let the ice cold wind flow
through every part of my being. I miss you so much, Charles.

Gotta go,

Professor K.

BIPOLAR GIRL

by Mickey Randleman

I was always drawn to duality.
My favorites were the ones with the worst conflicts:
The Hulk, trapped inside the cage of Dr. Banner,
Bruce Wayne's revenge masquerading as Batman's justice,
Jean Grey and her Dark Phoenix.
I loved the battles waged inside,
the barely contained forces that threatened to tear them apart,
the thin line between hero and villain.

I know what it's like to live in two halves,
I just never wore a mask.
Instead, drew "Normal" over my shoulders every day
like a cloak of invisibility.

None of my caped crusaders look like me.
They have origin stories full of gamma bomb malfunctions,
top-secret weapons projects, genetic mutations, rings of power;
My heroes made accidents into miracles.
My doctors made me into an accident.

I am ready for a real superhero,
someone who can tear the stigma off mental illness with their bare hands,
set the DSM-V on fire from across a room,
and fly far, far above this straitjacket skyline.

I think the world is ready for...
Bipolar Girl!
A super heroine who truly never sleeps--
at least for a few weeks at a time.
A woman who can run as fast as her pressured speech,
can punch through solitary confinement walls,
and manipulate reality with merely a thought.

I am ready to take up the mantle,
don the thigh high boots of righteousness,
name my left hook mania and my right jab depression,
and harness my mood swings for the benefit of all humanity.
I am ready to stand proudly upon the peak of human achievement
and proclaim:

Mental illness is a burden that gives us superhuman strength.
We walk among you, invisible inside our mild-mannered alter egos,

but we are fighting the villains inside our skin
every day.

Just let me be the hero of my own story.

MYSTIQUE: THE LAST DANCE

by Grae Rose

To my beloved friend,

You have been gone from me
for some time now.
You know me,
I am not superstitious.
Cosmic connections are
more your area of expertise.
But I have the strangest feeling
that you can hear me
from wherever you've gone.
So here it goes.

Irene, when you died,
our love was nearly
a century old.
We spent so much time hiding,
outcast both as mutants
and as lovers, forced to
put on an act of normalcy
for those who would do us harm.
Luckily, facades are my specialty.
The time I spent with you
as Mr. Raven, every time
I became a man to be
close to you in public,
it meant no less to me,
because even though
my body had changed,
I was still me,
and I was with you.

I have always thought of myself
as quicksilver,
changing with every heartbeat,
impossible to hold.
But you held me, tightly.
I never wanted you to let go.
You saw me only in your mind's eye,
impervious to my charms and tricks.
All you ever saw was me.
The true me.
I cherished you for that.

You must have known there would come a time
when people who love the way we did
would no longer have to hide themselves.
You had a softer place in your heart
for the humans than I ever did.
I can't pretend that I feel any more
deeply for them now, but I do
like the thought of asking you to dance,
in a crowded room,
wearing my true body,
pressed into your arms.

You asked me to enjoy life when you were gone,
to revel in it, as I was never able to do while you were alive.
But I resisted you.
How could I imagine being happy
ever again after losing you?
We built a home together.
We raised a beautiful daughter together.
When you foresaw I would have nightmares,
you got up early to share in coffee and comfort.
You were my only real friend,
my best friend, and more wonderful
a partner than I had ever dared to hope for.
And then, miles apart,
I heard your death scream.
I felt you die.

Others have criticized you for failing
to use your powers to protect yourself,
but I know, you did this for me.
You died to save me.
I may never forgive myself for this.
I know you saw that, too.
But I know I would have done the same.

In the end, you got the last laugh,
didn't you, Irene?
You finally made me laugh.
And you know what?
You're right.
For all my nihilism,
all my struggling against the futures
you knew were cut in crystal,
all my rage and torment,
all the time I've spent mourning you,
life goes on.
Even when you don't want it to,
even when it hurts,
even when you aren't part of it anymore,
life goes on.

I never saw the way you could,
kept razor sharp focus on single threads
while you admired the entire tapestry.
Sometimes it was hard for me to accept
that you saw farther than I did.
But, with your help,
I think I'm beginning to see.

Obla-dee, obla-da, life goes on…

I love you, Irene.

But you knew that,
even before I did,
didn't you?

THUS SPOKE AQUAMAN

by Steve Ramirez

You think of me as that fishy guy in the corner.

O, ye of little faith.

I am:
three-quarters of the whole ball of wax, like the inverted section of an iceberg… you do remember what icebergs meant to the Titanic, don't you?

I am:
the lifeblood of this planet. You chose the air, while I swim beneath a liquid sky and I have learned to dance the currents of the air.

I am:
storms waiting. Consider me Hurricane Orin, or Bob, or Jane; the rage of the ocean battering your coastlines, an early warning system for the lurking ecological disaster you've been brewing for years.

I am:
a Dark Rider on a pale seahorse, knocking on your door at 3 am, while my pestilent waves seep through your sprinklers and the other Horsemen of the Apocalypse are busy tuning up their Sea-Doos… you assume that the Riders of the Storm will be seen and heard on the tiny islands you scamper across while we float beneath the surface.

I am:
watching everything you do. You see me as a fish out of water, but I am the ultimate amphibious assault unit, and have no need for guns, or video-guided missiles… the violence of the sea is hidden behind the placidity of my eyes: Shamu is a killer whale; Orca, the living embodiment of the hunter, ready to tear and thrash you poor little seals in your cruise ships and submarines—tuna comes in a can and so do you, but we don't need a can opener—we of the sea have shark's teeth and are prepared to bite; we do not rely on our eyes to prove what we know to be true; we smell where you are and what you know; we hear where you've been and where you'll go; I shout my name into the Mariana Trench and it echoes back as 'Patience.' There's a reason you make so many films about the sea and why each one scares you. There's a formula behind your dreams of drowning and the uneasy look you get when your child swims too far from shore and the gentle scream of waves turns into the heartbeat of our common mother twisting into drums beating the warpath becoming the reverent thrum of your innocence being shattered while you wonder *why? Why me? Why now? Why didn't we learn?*

I am:
Noah.
I am:
Jonah.

I am:
Poseidon.

I am:
deeper than you imagine,
stronger than you can conceive,
darker than you think.

I am:
your gills, abandoned.

I am:
your lungs, filled with water.

I am:
each one of you,
suddenly remembering
how to breathe.

SUPERHERO

by Theresa Davis

I have been on this planet for more than just a minute
and I had gotten to that point where I thought I had heard
just about everything, when my six year old son comes to me,
finger extended looking very serious,
like he's going to point me out. He's on to me
knows I have no idea what I am doing, and he says to me

Mom, when you cut my fingernails this low
I can't pick my nose right
And I want to laugh but I don't. Instead I ponder
the digit as seriously as he is, and I say
You know what son, you're right. Now I know.

And he nods and walks away,
and I start doing the mommy Jedi mind trick thing, thinking
baby wash your hands, and I think he's heard me
because he stops at the bathroom door but then he turns,
bypasses the bathroom, comes to me with another question, and he says

Mom, if you were a superhero
and you had to wear tights
what color tights would they be?

HA! Like I would be caught dead wearing tights, so me being me
I say the most outrageous thing I can think of: I put my hands on my hips,
I throw my head back and I say,
Pink baby! Your momma would wear pink tights!

And he nods and walks away and I'm still thinking *baby wash your hands*
but it makes the questions he asked the previous week now make sense
like when he asked

Mom, do you remember that night when it was three o'clock in the morning, and
the fan in my sisters' room caught on fire and they were screaming like girls, and
you weren't awake, and your hair was loose, but you picked up the flaming fan
stepped in melted plastic and metal, burned your foot three degrees, put the fan
out in the tub, and made us go back to bed?

and I was really hoping he wouldn't remember that
but I say yes, I remember and he said *That was super*
or when he asked
Mom, do you remember that time when we were driving in the car
and a Christmas tree came, and it smashed our car up, and we didn't die
Mom, do you remember when we didn't die?

and I say *yes, I distinctly remember us not dying*
and he said *That was super so,*
when the tug on my sleeve bringing me back to the present
I feel the dampness on his hand. The mommy Jedi mind trick works.
And he says *Mom, I'm going to wear blue tights.*
Sidekicks can wear blue can't they, Mom?
And I get it. My son thinks I'm super
but what I want him to remember always is that he is my hero.

MULTIVERSE ASSEMBLE!

The roll call of justice, as penned by the poets themselves!

Jeff Austin
Jeff Austin is a government experiment resulting from applying CRT radiation to an impressionable sugar-fueled mind.

David Ayllon
When threatened, David Ayllon can fall into a deep slumber, resembling death, to confuse his enemies.

A. Bissa
If there's a planet that produces loudmouth pop-music-devotee Amazons, A. Bissa was born there and immediately thereafter named their empress.

Rich Boucher
Born with HDTV, Rich Boucher possesses approximately one times the strength of the average adult male who rarely exercises, and he has the power of "midcognition", the ability to see things and events that are right in front of him.

John F. Buckley & Martin Ott
After being viciously snuggled by a radioactive onesie, John F. Buckley gained the proportionate strength and speed of fleece sleepwear.

Kieran Collier
Kieran Collier is able to love Tobey Maguire as Spider-Man, and that is a super power in itself.

Theresa Davis
When she cracked from her egg on Planet Sappho, Theresa Davis emerged if full pirate regalia ready for any poetic situation. Her goal to run-through all bullshyt in her path. You know she is there when you hear her battle cry, "Prepared to be Boarded!"

Dalton Day
Dalton Day was born into a house of many bears and can cry at the speed of light.

Kathleen Delaney-Adams
Able to leap tall buildings in 5-inch stilettos, Kathleen Delaney-Adams makes the girls weep and the boys long for...well, no one is quite sure.

Susan Dobbe Chase
Wonder Woman's exploits have thrilled and inspired many young girls, including Susan Dobbe Chase.

Stevie Edwards
Editors' Origin: Stevie Edwards has the uncanny ability to assemble bursts of cosmic light into poem form and make arch-villains exclaim Good Grief in an non-ironic fashion. Xavier's School for Gifted Youngsters has her on the short list for teaching positions.

Karen Garrabrant
Karen G. is alive in the already apocalyptic Pyrothon, busily honing her skill of transforming toxic waste into renewable energy.

Joanna Hoffman
Joanna Hoffman possesses the power of Cat Telepathy and often calls on the felines of New York City to rescue her from stalled F trains, obnoxious tourists, and piles of dirty laundry. At this time, all distress calls have gone unanswered.

Victor Infante
Victor D. Infante is just a myth whispered in the darkened alleyways, isn't he?

Gary Jackson
Everything I've read tells me that you never announce your real superpower, since your enemies could exploit that knowledge against you, so I'll just say my superpower is the ability to not talk while watching television.

Geoff Kagan Trenchard
Geoff Kagan Trenchard is a thriving transplant to Gotham City and can complete law school while raising two small children in a single bound.

Lindsay King-Miller
Lindsay King-Miller has the proportional haircut of a lesbian and the ability to decipher any handwriting, no matter how terrible.

Zachary Kluckman
Zachary Kluckman stalks the streets of Albuquerque metaphysically, from his window, with truly cosmic powers of observation and introversion - and an uncanny knowledge of Ginger Ale.

The Klute
The Klute, who has received more than his share of accolades and gets along nicely with the rest of humanity, was NOT injured in that lab accident. His turn to supervillainy is considered kind of a dick move.

Heather Knox
Heather Knox woke during a midwestern thunderstorm able to harness the powers of Shabby Chic for good. She isn't the other Heather Knox.

David Doc Luben
Doc Luben sometimes wakes up as a giant. This is not the reason his bed is broken.

Kim Marshall
Exposed to the Aurora Borealis at a delicate age, Kim Marshall now zips around the world, traveling on light beams with stealth, colorful insights, and fabulous shoes.

Ryk McIntyre
Ryk McIntyre has had more than enough time to prepare. He is Batman. This argument was over before it even began.

Stephen Meads
Having spent his formative years on the surface of planet Pondera, Stephen Meads now thinks his way through all of life's dilemmas as the Introspect!

Curtis X Meyer
Curtis X Meyer can't help that he was born this way.

Eric Morago
Trying to save a puppy, Eric Morago fell into a vat of gamma-whiskey and was transformed into a bourbon-skinned behemoth, who now smashes straws in whiskey drinks across the land. (What the hell was a puppy doing at a distillery?)

David Ohlsen
The smirking shapeshifter known locally as David Ohlsen was banished to earth after unsuccessfully impersonating the King of the Galaxy.

Jennifer-Leigh Oprihory
The product of a police officer and a psychic, Jennifer-Leigh Oprihory is a human lie-detector and journalist who uses her power, pen and an enchanted compass to teleport around the world and fight crime.

Mark Palos
Due to a failed experiment to change the past, Mark was marooned in this time. In an attempt to salvage what good he can from the fact that he is stuck in a time not his own, uses the only tool at his disposal: poetry. He dreams of one day roaming the wasteland of a post-apocalyptic future in a modified Mustang on an endless search for gasoline...

Jesse Parent
Jesse Parent erupted fully formed from the fluffy brow of a Mentat and uses his adamantium tipped eyebrows to serve up sassy slicing stares to internet trolls and long winded SlamMasters.

Chad Parentau
Chad Parenteau was gifted with the proportionate social and professional track record of a misanthrope that bit him when he was a teenager, only to find out that the misanthrope wasn't radioactive, just really really sick.

Alan Passman
Minding his own business, Alan Passman wandered into a barren patch of California desert when he saw a great light made of the essence of long ago eaten Fruit Loops that bombarded him, giving him strange new powers, and that's when he became Passman, Drinker of Sparkling Water.

Baruch Porras-Hernandez
Baruch Porras-Hernandez is a mutant but was rejected from the Jean Grey School for Gifted Youngsters because of his uncontrollable power to give all the straight dudes within a four mile radius of him, boners. 4 hour boners. That only settle down when Baruch eats gummy bears. There were never enough gummy bears.

Robbi Ramirez
When Disney officials tried to use DNA from Walt's frozen head to clone an heir to the throne of Orlando, a terrible accident involving a sample of R. Crumb's semen led to the birth of a hideous ape-man who reads nothing but comic books and the occasional Palahniuk novel.

Steve Ramirez
Faster than a tall building! Able to leap speeding train tracks in a series of mighty skips! Steve Ramirez spends his days masquerading as a small print shop, but at night he dons his bath towel cape and Star Wars pajamas to battle evil as the high flying El Lunch Box, Protector of Truth, Justice and Spare Change!

Mickey Randleman
The sole survivor of a childhood plagued by horrifying experiments and torture, Mickey Randleman emerged with an armor-plated heart, an emotional invisibility cloak, and an undying vow to smash sexism wherever it may lurk.

Grae Rose
Grae Rose was born with a superhuman sense of anxiety and spends her days taking down evil-doers with strongly worded Post-It notes and scathing puns.

Patricia Smith
Editors' Origin: Patricia Smith's superpower is being Patricia Smith. No, really. Look it up.

Rob Sturma
Rob Sturma was rocketed from Planet Emo equipped with a sad mixtape and the ability to hold up a boombox over his head in a sweeping cinematic gesture for at least the duration of one Peter Gabriel song.

Hannibal Tabu
Hannibal Tabu was delivered by stealth to ordinary mortal parents who could do nothing to deter his mission of ending all humanity.

Robbie Q. Telfer
Robbie Q. Telfer was born in the knot of a tree stump and can sulk for justice.

Ben Trigg
Bathed in a lifetime of ambient radiation emanating from Disneyland, Ben Trigg's beard is now the happiest place on earth.

Leigh White
Leigh-thal Leigh White uses sarcasm like a clown car and has the ability to give anyone that goes over the 3 poem/5 minute rule an instant case of explosive diarrhea using mind bullets and the music of Creed.

Wonder Dave
Wonder Dave received the news of his super powers from a dentist. The dentist told him that not only were all the years of grinding in his teeth really bad for him, they had also left him with over developed jaw muscles and the bite strength of a pit bull.

Gus Wood
Gus Wood, an undead Trapeze Artist, spills his guts and uses them to swing to the rescue.

Scott Woods
Scott Woods takes great pride in being one of only a handful of black superheroes whose title doesn't start with the word "Black." Super Friends, indeed.

If You Loved MultiVerse, MultiVerse Loves . . .

Birthday Girl with Possum
by Brendan Constantine

The Year of No Mistakes
by Cristin O'Keefe Aptowicz

Slow Dance with Sasquatch
by Jeremy Radin

Everyone I Love Is A Stranger To Someone
by Anneleyse Gelman

This Way To The Sugar
by Hieu Nguyen

Write Bloody Publishing distributes and promotes great books of fiction, poetry, and art every year. We are an independent press dedicated to quality literature and book design, with an office in Austin, TX.

Our employees are authors and artists, so we call ourselves a family. Our design team comes from all over America: modern painters, photographers, and rock album designers create book covers we're proud to be judged by.

We publish and promote 8 to 12 tour-savvy authors per year. We are grass-roots, D.I.Y., bootstrap believers. Pull up a good book and join the family. Support independent authors, artists, and presses.

Want to know more about Write Bloody books, authors, and events?
Join our mailing list at

www.writebloody.com